Guaranteed to Fail

Socialism does not work, because socialism cannot work.

By

George E. Anderson, III, PhD

George E. Anderson, III, PhD

ISBN: 9781717802910

Acknowledgements

Like all authors, I owe a debit of gratitude to the people who worked to perfect my efforts. My beloved wife, Bell K Anderson who is fondly referred to as my 'comma Nazi'; my son, C. Schuyler Anderson who worked diligently to improve his father's work; and Major James Mallinson, good friend and English tyrant, who knows more about our native language than most editors; and many others who were encouraging and helpful along the way.

Like many works, this is a compilation and a synthesis of the work which came before me. I am intellectually indebted to F.S. Hayek, Laurence J. Peter, Vilfredo Pareto, C. Northcote Parkinson, and others.

George E. Anderson, III, PhD

Dedication

I would like to dedicate this work to the brave men and women who have defended America, from its creation in 1776 until today.

John 15:13:

'Greater love hath no man than this, that a man lay down his life for his friends.'

CONTENTS

Prologue   i

1 The Nature of Man   Page 1

2 Defining Socialism   Page 8

3 The Slave Contract   Page 18

4 Who decides what is 'good'   Page 21

5 Applied Social Psychology   Page 23

6 The Need for a Bureaucracy   Page 31

7 Parkinson's Law   Page 38

8 The Peter Principle   Page 42

9 Pareto Distribution   Page 47

10 Process   Page 50

11 Atrophy & Collapse   Page 59

12 Hope   Page 63

13 Addendum   Page 66

George E. Anderson, III, PhD

Prologue

The concept of socialism has been with the world since Plato's Republic. Plato envisioned a highly ordered society, broken down into three classes, where everyone had a purpose and was content to perform the role society assigned to each; Producers (such as craftsmen, farmers, artisans), Auxiliaries (warriors), and Guardians (rulers). It would be a benevolent state run for the benefit of all citizens by the superior, wise, and moral Guardians. Unfortunately, it never works out that way.

'Socialism in general has a record of failure so blatant that only an intellectual could ignore or evade it.' - Thomas Sowell

The modern strain of socialism was born in Europe during the 19th century. It was a time of social and economic dislocation. Changes in agricultural production and the early industrial revolution created great suffering for many. Philosophers, like Hagel, Engles, Weber, and Marx combined to create the concept of Socialism, which looked very much like Plato's Republic in which a class of wise, moral, selfless, individuals would rule for the benefit of all citizens.

The modern realization of socialism came into existence with the Bolshevik Revolution in Russia. The Bolsheviks seized power to create a fair and equitable society, without the residual medieval hierarchy of the Romanov dynasty or the greedy free markets of the capitalist system. A fair and equitable society, in which workers, through the governmental ownership of the means of production, would bring the benefits of that production equitably to the entire society and not to a few individuals. 'From each according to his ability, to each according to his need!' or in current terms 'Social Justice' was the socialists battle cry.

This beguiling concept spread during the 20th century across much of the globe; taking hold in Russia (later the Union of Soviet Socialist Republics), China, North Korea, Vietnam, Cambodia, Cuba, across Eastern Europe, Africa, Central and South America. In each case it was accompanied by waves of social upheaval, mass murder, and deprivation. In his work, *Black Book of Communism*, Martin Malia estimates a death toll of between 85 and 100 million people directly and indirectly (Murdered by the state or died tangentially by acts of the state, i.e. the famine of the Great Leap Forward.) during the 20th Century. Similar patterns are being followed by the few remaining Communist / Socialist states of the early 21st Century. Cuba, North Korea, Venezuela all have socially and politically repressive regimes and economic deprivation.

Thus, with over a century of repeated failure at great cost in human suffering, why can we still find proponents of such a system? Typically, if the current proponents even admit to the historic horrors the response is 'The concept was simply not executed properly.' For them, the horrors of the 20th Century had to do with the execution of the concept not the actual flaws of the basic concept. Rubbish. This book is about why socialism and communism have always failed and are guaranteed always to fail.

Chapter 1

The Nature of Man

'Technology changes all the time; human nature, hardly ever.' -

Evgeny Morozov

From the early Greeks to today; a fundamental question has been 'What is the nature of man and can it change'? Anecdotal evidence is brought forth showing examples of both great nobility and great baseness within the same society and often within the same individual. The culmination of the Enlightenment with the American Revolution and its basis in individual rights is counter-balanced by the scourge of slavery. Individual dichotomy may be exemplified by the brilliance of Einstein marred by the despicable way in which he treated his first wife. Selfless service to others is an ideal which is more likely to be a selfish pursuit of personal wealth and glory. The fight between good and evil goes on in each of us every day.

A traditional liberal point of view is that man is a fallen creature. Individuals are (or can easily become) self-centered, greedy, and authoritarian. Therefore, no individual, no matter how seemingly noble can be trusted with too much power. Power corrupts, absolute power corrupts absolutely.

If that point of view is accurate, the only way to protect a free society is to ensure a government structured to limit the power of any individual or group. Within the American experience, the Founding Fathers carefully structured a three-branch government, in which the powers of government were separate, distinct, and easily at odds. No one branch, no one individual, could assume all the power. The Balance of Powers was born to restrain fallen man.

That, of course, does not prevent politicians from acts of corruption and abuse of power. But having power diffused with multiple competitive forces, does restrain corruption. Pointing out the corruption of a political opponent has long been a traditional and effective tool for election.

For years, psychological theory believed that human personality was fixed, perhaps even genetically preordained. **(An Introduction to Behavior Genetics 1st Edition, 2008 by Terence J. Bazzett)** Along with the rise of socialism, there were those who argued, with work, individuals can alter their personalities; i.e. the shy becoming more gregarious and the selfish more giving. Leftist political theorists since Karl Marx have argued that the nature of man can be changed by changing the environment in which people live. By taking away the profit motive, one takes away individual greed. By fulfilling individual needs, (i.e. free education, medical care, food, housing.) one takes away fear. Through Social Engineering, that is by 'properly' structuring society, and providing socially acceptable societal inputs, a new type of human nature will emerge in which all the flaws of the human spirit, greed, envy, lust, fear disappear. As man is perfected; things such as war, poverty, and hunger will no longer plague mankind; all is possible if society is simply structured properly.

Two major psychologists have supported the concept of Social Engineering; Ivan Pavlov (classical conditioning), in the first half of the 20th Century, and B.F. Skinner (operant conditioning), in the latter half of the 20th Century. Lenin was quoted as saying Pavlov was the savior of the socialist revolution. In a conscience attempt to alter individual human nature Pavlov's experiments with salivating dogs could be expanded to gain support for his revolution. The Bolsheviks tried such techniques but later simply decided it was easier to murder anyone who did not share their world view. B.F. Skinner popularized the concept of operant conditioning. If one establishes a connection between a stimulus (either pleasurable or painful) and a behavior; you will generate a corresponding behavior. If every time the pigeon pecks the bar, it gets a pellet of food, the pigeon will soon spend his entire day pecking at the bar.

'The ideal of behaviorism is to eliminate coercion: to apply controls by changing the environment in such a way as to reinforce the kind of behavior that benefits everyone.' - B. F. Skinner

Skinner published his work 'Beyond Freedom and Dignity' in 1971. It became the basis for the academic discipline of Social Psychology (Social Engineering) and he became the darling of those who believed in the perfection of the individual by the government.

Thus we have the two opposing points of view: man is inherently flawed vs. man (societies) can be molded to an ideal. The two concepts could not be more diametric.

If man is inherently flawed, he will not become more virtuous by the acquisition of power. In fact, it is highly likely the addition of power will accentuate an individual's flaws and make them less virtuous. The less coercive power an individual can exercise over others, the more an individual must depend upon persuasion. It becomes less likely for abuse to occur. It logically follows then; the best government is the least government.

If however, one believes individuals and societies can be socially engineered into a paradise on earth, logically, we have two additional problems: firstly, who chooses what is 'good' and secondly, how is this 'good' imposed upon the rest of society? The pursuit of imposed perfection is inherently elitist. The elite decide what is good and then decide how to impose that good upon the rest of society.

'There are people out there who truly believe they are wiser and nobler than others (the anointed) and the way to improve society is for the government to force people to follow what the anointed want rather than let people do what they themselves want.' - Dr. Thomas Sowell Economist

How, then, do the self-anointed intend to 'guide' society towards perfection? The easiest and least expensive way is through voluntary cooperation. Provide sufficient stimulus through 'information,' taxes, and social pressures to move the society towards the pre-determined 'good.' Can this be achieved? Certainly; between 1939 and 1945, millions of Germans believing they were fighting for western civilization marched off to war.

However, 'improving' society is inherently coercive. If acquiescence of the lower classes cannot be achieved through persuasion, then for the good of 'society' we must coerce those who are not inclined towards the new 'good.' Those who could not be persuaded to be supportive of the goals established by the anointed (Nazis) or were deemed by the elite to be unworthy of the new society, were marginalized or simply liquidated. The more perfect a society we wish to create, the more coercion we must be willing to impose.

In more radical socialist revolutions (Cuba, Cambodia, Russia) the new ruling elite of the Communist party found spending the time attempting to use persuasion to gain compliance was too much effort. Purging their respective societies of undesirables via mass murder was simple and effective.

Please note; there are certainly legitimate roles for governmental activity: maintaining the peace, common defense, enforcement of contracts, some public services, and basic scientific research.

Thus, our choice of limited government or big government is tied to our belief in the perfectibility of mankind. If we believe man is fundamentally flawed, men and government must be restrained. If we believe man is fundamentally malleable and all we need is the right people to make decisions and the right formula of social tools (including mass murder) to form them, then we should believe in large government. History and humanity would lead us to choose the former, not the latter.

Chapter 2

Defining Socialism

'Socialism is a philosophy of failure, the creed of ignorance, and the gospel of envy, its inherent virtue is the equal sharing of misery.' - **Winston Churchill**

Today the dictionary defines socialism as 'a th eory or system of social organization that advocates the vesting of the ownership and control of the means of production and distribution, of capital, land, in the community as a whole.' Classically, it is simply government ownership of everything. However, there are multiple branches of the same tree.

The most radical, and humanly damaging, is Communism or International Socialism. There are those who have claimed that Communism is not Socialism, but that is simply not accurate. The complete name for the Soviet Union was 'The Union of Soviet Socialist Republics'. The government owned everything and controlled everything. It is true; the Communist propensity for the immediate murder of anyone who might disagree with their policies made them the worst strain of socialism.

Fascism; or National <u>Socialism</u>, had a propensity for violence which was only marginally less than the Communist regimes of the 20th century but there was less economic disruption, in that fascist regimes tended toward economic control rather than economic ownership. So long as the government controlled all economic activity, dictating labor conditions, product development, corporate profit margin the economic difference between a fascist and a communist was a distinction without a functional difference. (The geo-political difference between the two: being international socialist government vs. national socialist government.)

A third strain of socialism, which is popular today amongst both academics and leftist political types, is 'Democratic Socialism'; the greatest good for the greatest number being established through the ballot box, without violence. Like fascism, a carefully regulated private sector is the hallmark of Democratic Socialism. Countries such as Denmark, Sweden, Iceland and until recently Venezuela have been held up as shining examples of the success of Democratic Socialism. At least some of the Danes seem to disagree (http://www.investors.com/politics/commentary/denmark-tells-bernie-sanders-to-stop-calling-it-socialist/)

There are those who allege that because Fascists and Democratic Socialists do not advocate the complete assumption of the means of production by government, they are by definition **not** socialists. By strict interpretation I would agree. However, by the resulting nature, I would disagree.

There are certain industries in which government-controlled monopolies make sense. An example, would be the general category of utilities, such as water companies, and power distribution companies. It would simply not be practical to have multiple water companies running lines attempting to serve the same neighborhoods; thus, government control is needed. The tacit agreement is the government provides protection in the marketplace for a supplier in exchange for functional control of its business. The regulated company is required by the government to perform certain functions, mostly in the development and delivery of their product, with a limited ability to raise rates. In exchange, the government generally guarantees the ROI (Return on Investment) of the utility company. The government does not own the utility company; it simply controls everything the company does.

Whether compliance to governmental dictates is by consent or coercion, whether the means of production is directed or all property is owned by the state; all three forms of socialism carry the same implications. #1 Socialism is elitist. One of the great questions facing socialism is 'Who decides what is good?' According to socialism, government should be controlled by select, superior (usually self-appointed) people. They will make decisions for the good of everyone, based upon their 'superior ability,' knowledge, and moral virtue. It follows then; those not of the ruling class are inherently inferior. They are incapable of making enlightened decisions for themselves. They need and should welcome protection and direction.

Of course, personal superiority of those in power is a myth. People do not become more moral, wiser, or more diligent when given power. Chances are extremely good that just the opposite is true.

#2 Socialism is inherently corporate; limiting or eliminating the significance of the individual. The needs of 'The People' replace the desires of 'The Individual'. The designated welfare of the many is more important than the welfare of the few. One can see this in the architecture of socialist states. Public buildings tend to be huge, impressive, and largely useless. Private buildings, such as apartment housing, tends to be much smaller and asigned based on need.

During the building of the J.V. Stalin Moscow-Volga Canal in Russia it is estimated Stalin used over 100,000 people, many political opponents of the state, others simply drafted off the streets of Leningrad. Officially, over 12,000 died during the construction. ((Moscow: Permanent interdepartmental commission of the Moscow Government to reestablish the rights of rehabilitated victims of political oppression, 1998) pp. 32-42.) The needs of the many (or at least the desires of the dictator) were more important than the lives of the few.

The same pattern was followed with almost every other socialist state; Hitler's, great public works, and the Romanian socialist dictator Nicolae Ceaușescu spent billions on public buildings, the monuments 'to the people.' Socialist architecture is intended to impress the importance of the state and the insignificance of the individual.

#3 Socialism is inherently coercive: 'the greatest good for the greatest number,' with the dissenting few forced into tolerating the will of the ruling class. If we vote on it, if our ruling elite decide it is 'good' and in the best interest of 'the people' and it is to your personal detriment, well tough; comply or perish.

Most people clearly understand the Nazi Holocaust was

the logical result of ethnic cleansing. Few recognize the same process was used to eliminate any political dissent in Germany. Oppose almost any socialist regime and off to the camps.

#4 Socialism kills 'truth.' One of the very first things that dies during the introduction of socialism is 'truth.' The easiest way of gaining compliance is through persuasion. The truth is irrelevant. The intellectual elite are entitled to use whatever deceit is required to bring voluntary compliance with their vision of the socialist paradise.

In the United States, a good example of this was when Pres. Obama was promoting his universal healthcare bill. The American people were made a series of promises, which proved not to be true.

'I will sign a universal health-care bill into law by the end of my first term as president that will cover every American and cut the cost of a typical family's premium by up to $2,500 a year.' 'If you like your doctor or health care provider, you can keep them. If you like your health care plan, you can keep that, too.' - Pres. Obama

The statements were clearly false. It is hard to determine whether they were deliberate deceptions, but if it was a deliberate lie, it was for the 'greater good' so the ends justified the means. And according to precept #1, the elite not only have the right to impose their vision on others, they have the moral obligation to do so.

'But we have to pass the bill so you can find out what is in it.'- Nancy Pelosi

The arrival of a socialistic system of government comes in two forms: 'revolutionary' and 'creeping'. Revolutionary socialism can be either legal, as in the election of a socialistic government, as in Chile in 1970 or Venezuela in 1998, or extra-legal, as in the violent overthrow of an existing government, such as in Russia in 1917 or China in 1949. In each case a new self-defined socialist government is put into power with the purpose of bringing about as much social change as possible in the minimum time possible. Laws are decreed or passed by the self-appointed elite. Property is confiscated in the name of 'fairness', the means of production is nationalized, or strict oversight is instituted. Government is expanded and anyone objecting is violently suppressed.

Creeping socialism has occurred in many Western nations. Over a period of years, the government takes on a larger role in the society. Often, some form of tragedy occurs and citizens demand governmental action to prevent such a thing from reoccurring. A mine collapses, miners are killed and the citizens demand the government protect miners with new legislation and regulation. A plane crashes, people demand the government do something to prevent such a horror from happening again. It all sounds totally reasonable, but as we shall see, what starts as a good idea takes on a life of its own.

While the 2016 election may have signaled a significant shift in political philosophy of America, let me provide two examples of industries which were negatively impacted during the Obama years by government regulation.

Tangier Island in the Chesapeake Bay has a long history going back to the 1670s. Until recently depended the islands upon two industries; soft shell crabs and tourism. For those who live away from the Chesapeake Bay, a soft shell crab is one of the true delicacies of life, and people pay a premium for them. They are hard to produce and the market is small.

There are still several wonderful bed and breakfasts on the island; however, but the soft shell crab business has been almost completely shut down. Why? During the Obama administration, agents from the Federal Government arrived and placed a series of regulations upon the islanders' soft-shell crab business which simply could not be economically met. The last time we visited Tangier Island, there was a noticeable shortage of adult males. We were told all the men had all gone 'Tugging' (working on seagoing tugboats) to make a living because the new regulations covering soft shell crabs made it impossible to earn a living in that way.

The second and much larger example of governmental intrusion is the coal industry. It was the stated objective of the Obama administration that through the use of government regulation they would kill the coal industry. Coal was seen by those in the administration as a major contributor to global warming, and they simply decided to place complex and unattainable regulations on the industry in hopes of killing it. Mines were shut down, and thousands of people (perhaps tens of thousands) were unemployed and impoverished.

New Carbon Rules the Next Step in Obama's War on Coal – Time Magazine
http://time.com/2806697/obama-epa-coal-carbon/

It was a classic example of government's not needing to own the means of production, (if it can control the means of production) to meet the goal of the self-appointed elite. Under the Trump administration many of the regulations burdening the coal industry are being eliminated and the industry is returning to economic viability.

Bureaucracy Kills: A Lesson from Rome - William Henry Chamberlin

https://fee.org/articles/bureaucracy-kills-a-lesson-from-rome/

Chapter 3

The Slave Contract

'Emancipate yourselves from mental slavery, none but ourselves can free our minds!' - **Marcus Garvey**

The concept of a contract when speaking of slavery at first seems ridiculous. There is no written contract when it comes to slavery; no there is not. There is however an implied social contract.

'Most Americans, no doubt, imagine the prewar South as a region so thickly dotted with immense plantations on which most of the black and white populations worked and lived. But, on the contrary, while slaves made up 40% of the total population of the South, only 25 percent of free families, most of them white, owned any slaves at all, and fully one-half of this minority (12.5%) held fewer than five slaves.' - Armisted Robinson,

The economics of slave ownership dictated that some sort

of social contract be established between owner and slave. Why?

A slave represented another set of hands on the farm. In economic terms they were a means of production. They were the John Deere combine of their age. Like a John Deere, they were expensive to buy and any owner wanted to get the most production for their money.

Having a broken down tractor does a farmer no good. Having a broken down slave does the slave holder no good. Only when they are working does the owner make money.

So the question then becomes, how does the slave owner gain compliance from the slave? If a slave holder owns 100 slaves, the use of threats and violence is economically viable. After all, if one slave is taken out of production it serves as an 'example' to the other 99, and, at worst, one has only lost 1/100 of one's production capacity.

Violence does not work, however, when a slave holder has only one slave. Why not? If the slaveholder has to use violence to motivate their single slave and that slave is physically unable to work, then that man has lost 100% of his additional production capacity.

To be a productive relationship, a social contract must be tacitly agreed to between slaveholder and slave. The contract was guaranteed by the implied threat of physical violence but the contractual exchange was more direct. The slave was to accept servitude and be compliant with the directives of the slave holder. In exchange, the slave holder would provide food, shelter, and safety. It was an exchange of liberty for security. It is exactly the same social contract offered by Midevil European nobility to their serfs and the self-appointed socialist elite to the members of their countrymen.

In exchange for compliance with the will of the government (slaveholder) the citizens (slaves) will have everything they need provided; free education, medicine, and retirement, security will all be provided. All the citizen has to do is comply with the directives provided. The burdens of individual choice and individual risk are exchanged for a guarantee of basic comfort and the illusion of equality. Being taken care of by someone who 'cares' is very attractive for many, even if it is at the cost of personal freedom.

'Private initiative disappeared; more and more the all-powerful imperial government was expected to look after everyone and attend to everything.' - Edward Gibbon

Chapter 4

Who decides what is 'good'

'Our criteria for deciding what's good and what's bad is very fickle, especially in this country.' - **Roberta Flack**

From the very beginning, a standard socialist slogan has been 'The Greatest Good for the Greatest Number.' The question rarely addressed has been, 'Who will decide what is good?' In countries with small homogeneous populations the answer may well be obvious to all citizens. Having the people of Iceland agree on any government action is certainly easier than getting the population of India or the United States to agree on anything. For a large complex country, the libertarian answer to the question might be 'Everyone decides for themselves what is good for them.' The initial socialist answer may well be 'We'll vote on it!'

The, 'We'll vote on it' response has two problems. In a large, diverse country, can every question of 'what's good' be put to a vote? Seems highly unlikely. The second problem is the inherent elitism within socialism. What if the people vote the wrong way?

From simple necessity 'everyone voting on the question' in a large diverse country becomes 'our elected representatives' voting on the question. The larger the pool of elected officials, the more likely an issue is referred to committee, then subcommittee, which then makes the actual decision on 'What is good' in line with the desires of the committee chairman.

'When any organizational entity expands beyond 21 members, the real power will be in some smaller body.' C. Northcote Parkinson

Have you ever seen a picture of the various gatherings of a communist / socialist government? There are thousands of 'representatives,' too many to actually come to a consensus. But there is an effective number of 'representatives' to return home and enforce the will of the state. The masses are not to be trusted and the socialist concept of 'everyone votes on what is good' very quickly becomes an act of a small number of elite individuals imposing their will.

Two good examples of a political elite actually fearing a popular vote was the 2016 Democratic primaries. The primaries were rigged in favor of Hillary Clinton against the challenger Bernie Sanders. When challenged in court, the official position of the Democratic Party was that their primary was a private election and they had no legal responsibility to conduct it fairly. That position was accepted by the court.

Additionally, the Democratic Party has a system of 'Super Delegates' or party insiders, who are not bound by their local constituents' selection and have sufficient numbers to disproportionately influence the choice of candidates at the Democratic Convention. Super Delegates can in fact negate the entire primary process of the Democratic Party.

In 2016, the bottom up process of Democrats voting on what (or who) is good, quickly became a top down process with the elite of the party defining and enforcing who was 'good'.

If a small group of self-appointed elite individuals are going to decide what is good for the entire population, what will happen to those who disagree? The first step would be to attempt to gain their consent through persuasion or Applied Social Psychology.

Chapter 5

Applied Social Psychology

'Social psychology is especially interested in the effect which the social group has in the determination of the experience and conduct of the individual member.' -

George Herbert Mead

In the early 1900 Russian psychologist Ivan Pavlov began working on his theory of 'Pavlovian Conditioning' in which a dog could be conditioned to salivate when presented with a specific stimulus. The dog would hear a bell, be given a piece of food, and begin to salivate. After a series of such events, the food would be removed from the equation. The dog would hear the bell and begin to salivate. The bell was a voluntary stimulus (someone decided to ring the bell) but the response of salivation was an involuntary response (the dog did not decide to salivate).

There is a famous story that after reviewing his research Vladimir Lenin approached Pavlov, shook his hand and congratulated him on 'Saving the Revolution!! Why?

Guaranteed to Fail

Marx's concept of the selfless individual is a fraud. The fundamental needs of the individual and a seemingly unquenchable need for acquisition makes members of the human species egocentric. Thus socialism has the fundamental problem of running against human nature. Lenin thought the research which caused Pavlov's dogs to salivate could be applied to social settings creating conditioned, politically acceptable, behavior in 'the masses.'

In the late 1930s, the psychologist B.F. Skinner developed his theory of 'operant conditioning'; it means roughly changing of behavior by the use of reinforcement, which is given after the desired response. By rewarding some behavior and punishing other behaviors, individual actions can be adjusted. In his work; 'Beyond Freedom and Dignity' (1971) Skinner set out how the principles of operant conditioning could be applied not just to individuals but to entire societies. He believed that his research pointed the way to Marx's 'selfless man' and the perfect society.

Today, Skinner's social engineering is called by the more benign sounding name of Social Psychology and institutes of higher learning across America are awarding degrees in

Beyond Freedom & Dignity by B.F. Skinner.
ISBN-10: 0394425553, ISBN-13: 978-0394425559

the subject. Thousands are graduating each year, convinced they are among the intellectual, moral elite. They pride themselves with their ability to socially engineer entire societies never questioning if they have the right to impose their vision on other individuals.

Social engineers will point with pride to their various successes in American society: the reduction in the use of tobacco, the use of seatbelts, and the use of bicycle helmets each to the benefit of society. But each came with a corresponding reduction in individual liberty. The slave contract; do what you are told and everything will be great or don't do what you are told and suffer the consequences.

Making a decision as to 'What is good' when that decision is coming from a small group of elite individuals is comparatively easy. But with a large and complex society gaining universal compliance with the decision is vastly more difficult. Applied Social Psychology, social engineering, will certainly move a segment of the population (those who are comfortable with their slave contract) towards early acceptance of the good. While Social Psychology may not be able to move everyone to joyful acceptance, it can move a large segment of the population away from opposition towards tacit acceptance. ('I don't like it but what can I do?)

To be effective in altering the behavior of a group of people, Social Psychology needs to be fully implemented without challenge. A press story on the evils of XYZ loses its effectiveness if there is another article in another publication that expounds on the virtues of XYZ. To mold behavior, one needs to mold ideas, and conflicting points of view limit the effectiveness of that effort.

'Ideas are more powerful than guns. We would not let our enemies have guns, why should we let them have ideas.' - Joseph Stalin

Social psychology has many tools to influence social behavior. Those that pass today as journalists are often in fact activists attempting to advance a specific social agenda. Journalism used to be about presenting the 5 Ws: who, what, when, where, and why, with the personal opinion of the journalist being undiscernible. Today, many journalists are taught to 'Comfort the afflicted and afflict the comfortable.' They are activists for a particular social or political position. The blogger Dennis G. Jerz clearly states, 'It's now one of many pithy sayings I often used in my journalism classes.'

One of the favorite techniques is writing articles quoting

'scientific studies' and touting the validity of a position. For example, 'The New York Times, reported today on a study released by NYU, showing 95% of people disapprove of Pres. Trumps' handling of XYZ.' Few people will actually look for the study and fewer still will find out the study was done by asking students at NYU what they thought. Few will check the methodology, and fewer still are able to judge the validity of such a study, but the very fact the 'study' was conducted at a 'major university' gives credibility to the published conclusion.

'Thought Leaders' are another great tool of social psychology. Prominent public figures including athletes, actors, and TV personalities are often used to promote specific political points of view. Some endorsements by such people are blatant, some more subtle.

In 2009 Diane Sawyer of ABC News produced a 60-minute segment on the show 20/20 entitled 'If I Only Had A Gun.' She conducted an experiment as 'proof' that having a gun doesn't protect you and that having a gun would actually put an individual at higher risk. Diane Sawyer is a thought leader for millions of people, and her experiment was certainly taken as conclusive proof for many carrying a gun is a bad idea. Unfortunately, there were multiple and fatal flaws in the presentation. #1 the presentation was in fact a positive argument. There was no attempt to be balanced and present more than one side of the issue. #2 there were multiple logical errors in the experiment. It was simply rigged.

> You can see Diane Sawyer's presentation at;
>
> https://www.youtube.com/watch?v=ezzskoEB0Gc

There is nothing wrong with holding an opinion, but broadcasting a flawed 'experiment' as proof of that opinion is simply propaganda. It is an attempt to form public opinion. It is social engineering.

For those individuals who will not adopt the new 'right think' voluntarily, Laws can be written to coerce compliance with the new vision of good. The concept of 'Hate Crimes' is one such area. The Federal Bureau of Investigation defines a hate crime (also known as bias crime) as 'a criminal offense committed against a person, property, or society that is motivated, in whole or in part, by the offender's bias against a race, religion, disability, sexual orientation, or ethnicity/national origin.' Two major changes occurred to the Law under this definition. First, previously a crime was an 'act'. Under this definition, the crime is the 'motivation.' Secondly, motivated 'in whole or in part' raises the question, in whose perception?

For example; the burning of an American Flag is a protected form of free speech, but burning a Rainbow Flag is clearly a hate crime under the FBI definition. 49 states have adopted Hate Crime statutes, with 'Most states and large cities now have hate crime task forces coordinating across several levels of government and working with community organizations.' The thought police are active; disagree and face the wrath of the legal system... classic Applied Social Psychology / Social Engineering.

> National Institute of Justice, Office of Justice Programs; https://www.nij.gov/topics/crime/hate-crime/pages/welcome.aspx

Chapter 6

The Need for a Bureaucracy

'Bureaucracy is a giant mechanism operated by pygmies.' -

Honore' de Balzac

Some sort of government organization is required to carefully define and impose the new 'good' upon those who are hesitant to comply voluntarily. How is this organization going to be designed and staffed? Thus, government bureaucracy came into existence. (That is not to say government bureaucracy is an invention of the American government. The establishment of bureaucracies go back thousands of years: Egypt, Persia, Rome all had bureaucracies carrying out the will of the government.)

Bureaucracy is defined as: a body of unelected government officials, an administrative policy-making group, characterized by specialization of functions, adherence to fixed rules, and a hierarchy of authority. It is not unique to the United States, in fact every centralized government in human history has had some sort of bureaucratic structure. But how shall the bureaucracy be designed?

It the early days of the industrial revolution, efficiency was key to mass production. In 1909, Frederick Winslow Taylor published 'The Principles of Scientific Management.' His theory of scientific management conceived the management of a business, industry, or economy, should be conducted according to principles of efficiency derived from experiments in methods of work, especially from time-and-motion studies. Human activity was broken down into the smallest possible increments, and the most efficient of those elements was prescribed as THE way of production.

In an organization as large and complex as a government, scientific management would certainly seem to be a way to structure and control the bureaucracy. In most governments it is the system used to impose governmental will upon their citizens.

Some of these new 'goods' sound highly reasonable, some more radical, but all advance the socialist agenda of government control over the population. For example, almost everyone would accept clean water is a good thing. The bureaucracy is then legally charged with ensuring our water is clean. But what is the exact definition of clean water? Almost all water has various minerals dissolved in it. Which minerals are acceptable and which are not? At what levels are such minerals acceptable? How will those levels be measured? Who will be held responsible if there are violations? How will they be held responsible? The bureaucracy sets the definition of clean water, defines the water over which they have authority, and creates the tools they use to enforce the standards it developed. The more detailed the 'good' is, the larger the bureaucracy required to implement the vision.

'In any bureaucracy, there's a natural tendency to let the system become an excuse for inaction.' - Chris Fussell

To justify their existence, bureaucrats have an inherent need to exercise their authority. For example, in the late 1980s, the EPA brought charges against Eastman Kodak of New York. Eastman Kodak, had for almost a century provided thousands of jobs to the people of the Hudson valley. They had been socially engaged as a company, including providing grants to local schools and local family programs. They were proactive in seeking and complying with government standards for clean water. In many ways, Eastman Kodak was the model corporate citizen.

The production of photographic film is/was a chemical process. Many of those chemicals are toxic. Eastman Kodak was fully aware of this, fully disclosed the use of the chemicals and complied with government standards for their disposal. Then in the late 1980s, the Environmental Protection Agency (EPA) changed the rules.

Chemicals which had, with prior government approval, been disposed of by release into the Hudson river were no longer allowed to be disposed of in that way. Further, Eastman Kodak was responsible RETROACTIVELY for those chemicals which had been released into the Hudson river! The EPA directed that the length of the Hudson from the Eastman Kodak facilities south would have to be dredged and the residual chemicals removed. Not surprisingly, Eastman Kodak was to pay the financial costs of an estimated $1 Billion even though no one contested that Eastman Kodak had always operated within the regulations or that the chemicals which were buried in the river mud were not a current threat. (Later, good sense prevailed)

'The only thing that saves us from the bureaucracy is

its inefficiency.' -Eugene McCarthy

The expansion of the 'goods' a government defines, the greater the size of the bureaucracy required to deal with each function. It is good to have clean water. Under the Obama administration, federal government authority over water was expanded from navigable waterways to almost every source of water in the United States, including water barrels and fish ponds. The wider the definition, the greater the control and the more bureaucrats required to do the controlling.

'Bureaucracy defends the status quo long past the time when the quo has lost its status.' - Laurence J. Peter

It is a symbiotic relationship. The socialist elite define 'goods' and expand the bureaucracy to impose that 'good.' The bureaucracy supports the socialist elite, as new 'goods' provide them their very existence. It is good to have clean air. It is good to have safe cars. It is good to have higher education. It is good.. it is good... it is.... The more programs the government implements, the more people are required to oversee the programs.

There is a further challenge with governmental bureaucracies; through legislation, executive order, regulation, and union activity individual workers are insulated from any personal responsibility. After the uncovering of attempts to influence an American election by senior FBI officials, FBI director Christopher Wray announced he was going to implement a new round of 'retraining.' Under the existing rules, that seems to be the extent of his authority. Government employees are extremely difficult to fire. They can fail to act or even act in illegal ways, and it can still take years to terminate them.

From a bureaucrat's point of view, the bigger the bureaucracy the better. From society's point of view, perhaps not. Bureaucracies do not create wealth. At very best they reallocate the wealth others create.

'The number of ministers, of magistrates, of officers, and of servants, who filled the different departments of the state, was multiplied beyond the example of former times; and 'when the proportion of those who received exceeded the proportion of those who contributed the provinces were oppressed by the weight of tributes.' ... 'they unanimously agree in representing the burden of the public impositions, and particularly the land-tax and capitation, as the intolerable and increasing grievance of their own times.' – Edward Gibbon,

Bureaucracies are very good at protecting themselves. They are the natural ally of those who wish to expand government and the natural foe of anyone who wishes to reduce government.

Chapter 7

Parkinson's Law

'Work expands so as to fill the time available for its completion.'

The goal of any bureaucracy is its own preservation. That is achieved through its own expansion. One way to achieve that expansion is to expand the work required. Parkinson's Law applies to all human organizations, but especially to bureaucracies

'Work expands so as to fill the time available for its completion.' - C. N. Parkinson

If there is significant time allocated to a task in government, the task itself will expand. If the original question is 'How many people are there in California, now?', the question will immediately grow; 'How do we know?' "How does this compare to prior years?' 'What conditions are causing the change?' 'What are the political implications of the change?.'

A fair approximation of an answer to the initial question might be achieved by simply taking out one's phone and Googling it. But, such an approximation does not fulfill the need for bureaucratic expansion.

'The thing to be done swells in importance and complexity in a direct ratio with the time to be spent.' - C. N. Parkinson

Professional bureaucrats, to ensure their own positions and their career advancement really have two objectives; (1) 'An official wants to multiply subordinates, not rivals' and (2) 'Officials make work for each other.'
If an individual is overworked, he has three choices - #1: to quit the job, #2: to get some help and split the work or #3: to ask for two or more subordinates to do the same job. Few in the history of mankind have ever chosen anything but #3. Within an organization, the number of people you supervise is directly related to the authority and your income.

From the bureaucrat's point of view, it is important to 'staff' things. Staffing, or forwarding a document to everyone who possibly might have an opinion / input into the matter at hand allows two things to happen: #1 It creates 'work' and #2 it allows the originator to avoid personal responsibility if things go wrong (and take credit if things go right). The larger a bureaucratic organization, the more time managers spend 'staffing' and avoiding any actual productive effort.

A friend of mine, after retiring from the US Army as a Major, was hired as an intelligence analyst. He was welcomed, shown where the coffee break room was, and given his cubical and general topic of responsibility. Then he was left alone. For three months, he watched people come and go in the office, precisely on time, but with no visible accomplishments. At that time, he decided to write an opinion paper and he spent the next couple of weeks producing his first considered opinion paper. He had worked hard on his paper and looked on it with great satisfaction. <u>He was reprimanded by his supervisor.</u>

He was reprimanded for he had violated two principles of the office. #1 His opinion paper contained..... an opinion! He could be wrong! The supervisor went through his work line by line and changing structure and terms until the opinion paper was void of anything which might later be judged as wrong... or constructive. #2, He produced his opinion paper much too early in his career! He should not attempt to write anything again for at least a year.

Both are classic examples of bureaucratic behavior.

'Work (and especially paper-work) is thus elastic in its demands on time, it is manifest that there need be little or no relationship between the work to be done and the size of the staff to which it may be assigned.' - C. N. Parkinson

As work expands to fill the time allowed, the essential gives way to the supplementary and finally to the irrelevant. Of course, the expansion of 'work' quickly requires additional staff.

In the private sector, the necessity for making a profit holds down the creation of unnecessary functions. 'How does this add to our profitability?' is a real and important question. It is a question which is never asked in the public sector. Indeed, the question, 'Why are we doing this at all?' is rarely asked.

Parkinson: The Law Complete, by C. N. Parkinson
Publisher: Ballantine Books; Reissue edition (May 12, 1983)
ISBN-10: 0345300645 ISBN-13: 978-0345300645

Chapter 8

The Peter Principle

'In a hierarchy, every employee tends to rise to his level of incompetence.'

Parkinson's Law requires an ever-expanding workforce. The Peter Principle compounds that effect by ensuring an ever-decreasing quality of worker, (thus, reinforcing the need for even more individuals to accomplish the same task.)

There are lots of reasons, (ethical, morale, financial) to promote people internally. When considering individuals for promotion, leadership naturally tends to look first at their current performance. (Are they doing a good job? Then let's promote them!) Ultimately, this results in people being promoted to their highest level of incompetence. They are promoted until they cannot handle or can only marginally handle the job.

Guaranteed to Fail

This is not necessarily due to a lack of intent but rather an alternative skill set required for the higher position. An outstanding writer might prove to be a terrible editor; the skill set is simply different. A good teacher may be a poor administrator who is unfit to be a school principal. The skill set to succeed at one position within an organization can be and often is completely different from the skill set needed to succeed at another level.

In many instances, the individual will not display sufficient competence to be promoted to the next level but they also will not display sufficient incompetence to be fired. Thus as employees climb the corporate ladder, they ultimately reach a level they cannot handle. They have reached their level of incompetence, The Peter Principle.

'in most hierarchies, super-competence is more objectionable than incompetence.' He warned that extremely skilled and productive employees often face criticism, and are fired if they don't start performing worse. Their presence 'disrupts and therefore violates the first commandment of hierarchical life: the hierarchy must be preserved.' — Laurence J. Peter

Ultimately, The Peter Principle suggests 'in time, every post tends to be occupied by an employee who is incompetent to carry out the duties of their position and the real work is accomplished by those employees who have not yet reached their level of incompetence.

It is unlikely an incompetent manager is inclined to promote a talented, competent, junior employee. The junior employee will be viewed as a potential rival to the marginally competent manager; rather, an incompetent manager is more likely to set a competent junior employee up to fail because he is seen as a personal threat.

As an organization matures, the percentage of individuals reaching their level of incompetence increases and the efficiency of the organization declines. In the private sector, people are fluid. They move from company to company in search of improving their personal situation. If an organization does start to decline because individuals are not doing their jobs, it can be addressed through moving personnel around, bringing in fresh employees, and the demotion or termination of the incompetent. If the situation is left unaddressed, the organization becomes unprofitable and fails. It is very different in the public sector.

Guaranteed to Fail

'In time, every post tends to be occupied by an
employee who is incompetent to carry out its duties.'
— Laurence J. Peter

In government, most employees are protected both by the
rules of Civil Service AND by public unions. The methods
that organizations in the private sector use to restore
efficiency are almost impossible to implement in the
public sector even if there were a desire to do so. To
demote, reassign, or terminate any employee in the public
sector is highly complex, time consuming, and practically
impossible.

One manifestation of the Peter Principle, which occurs in
the public sector and not in the private sector, is the
'Screw up and move up' phenomenon. Because it is
almost impossible to fire incompetent employees in the
public sector, often the only way to actually move them
out of the position they currently hold is by **promoting**
them. Thus, in some cases individuals occupy positions
which are far above their level of incompetence.

Promotion within the public sector is highly formalized,
with most if not all hiring from within the civil service.
Individuals tend to rise to the level of their incompetence
and stay there. With declining productivity, the only way a

public organization is able to continue to achieve a consistent level of results is by growing the number of employees.

I knew an employee of the National Guard, who clearly hated being around anything military. He was competent in his position but clearly miserable. When I asked him why he kept his job, the reply came back; 'It's the only job I can find; they cannot fire me.' A few years later, he retired and was replaced by an individual who played video games most of the day. He knew that, as long as he was minimally acceptable, no one could fire him. The National Guard found it easier to hire an additional full-time employee to 'help' him do his job, rather than to go through the difficult process of getting rid of him. They thus rewarded him for his incompetence. The Peter Principle lead to an expanded bureaucracy.

The Peter Principle: Why Things Always Go Wrong – October 25, 2011, Publisher: Harper Business; (October 25, 2011), ISBN-10: 0062092065, ISBN-13: 978-0062092069

Chapter 9

Pareto Distribution

**The Pareto Principle (or 80-20 rule) says that 80% of output
is created by 20% of the workers.**

The Pareto Principle is derived from the Pareto distribution, created by Vilfredo Pareto an Italian economist, mathematician, and philosopher. His mathematical construct was used to illustrate that many things are not distributed evenly. Originally written to state that 20% of the population holds 80% of the wealth, it can be applied more universally.

Distribution of world GDP, 1989

Quintile of population Income

Richest 20%	82.70%
Second 20%	11.75%
Third 20%	2.30%
Fourth 20%	1.85%
Poorest 20%	1.40%

For example, it can be used to model any general situation where results are not evenly distributed. In the private sector it is often pointed out that the top 20% of workers produce approximately 80% of output, that 20% of the sales force produces 80% of the revenue, that 20% of the customers produce 80% of the orders. (Of course, these are rough estimates and vary from company to company, industry to industry.)

There are those on the Left who use Pareto distribution to prove the inequity of the free market system; the wealth is unevenly distributed. Relation is not causation.

Application of the Pareto distribution does clearly describe the lack of productivity of a bureaucracy. If 20% of the workers are responsible for 80% of the production, what happens to an organization which constrains or eliminates the productive 20%? The scientific management approach used to structure a bureaucracy does just that. Roughly, you get an organization which produces 25%-30% of what it should be producing.

'Bureaucracy kills people's ability to try new ideas.' - Walter O'Brien

Dr. Peterson uses a slightly different mathematical model for a Pareto distribution; the square root of the population produces 50% of the output, but his thought process is valid.

> Jordan Peterson, PhD the Pareto distribution;
>
> (https://www.youtube.com/watch?v=i0iL0ixoZYo)

Chapter 10

Process

'If you can't describe what you are doing as a process, you don't know what you're doing.' - W. Edwards Deming

One of the definitions of 'process' in Merriam-Webster is: 'a series of actions or operations conducing to an end.' In the days prior to the industrial revolution the process of creating a specific good was passed down from the trade master to the apprentice. There was little division of labor. An individual was responsible for and executed the entire process of creation; a cobbler made shoes from the selection of the hides to the final stitching of the sole. A smith made swords from the forging of the steel to the polishing of the blade and the attachment of the handle.

With the birth of the industrial revolution, the process of creation was segmented to increase standardization and create volume production. No longer was a single individual responsible for the entire process of product creation. Rather labor was divided into an interconnecting flow of repetitive specialized tasks with many people contributing to the production of a product. The culmination of such segmentation became popularly known as the 'assembly line.'

Process and standardization made greater production possible than ever before in human history. For example, if a master cobbler using traditional methodology could make 1 pair of shoes a week, then it would be logical that using that methodology, 10 master cobblers could produce 10 pairs of shoes per week. As the production process of shoes was standardized and organized, those same 10 individuals may well have become able to produce 20 perhaps even 50 pairs of shoes per day. Standardized processes created successful mass production, providing the world material wealth which had been inconceivable a few short centuries before.

There are two major concerns over such specialization. The first is as the complexity of organizational process increases it becomes less and less likely that any one individual is able to replicate the process in its entirely. (Today, a skilled individual may be able to create a pair of shoes, but it is highly unlikely one could find an individual who could create an automobile from iron ore.)

As a result, the process becomes more fragile. The production of ten master cobblers may be limited to what they can achieve individually, but when one cobbler becomes incapacitated, the other 9 simply keep producing. $1/10^{th}$ of the production is lost. In the case of 10 individuals working within a structured, standardized process, when one individual stops, the entire process breaks down, and 100% of the production is lost. While there are certainly steps which are taken to reduce the risk of breakdown, the more complex the standardized process is the more fragile it becomes.

Consider modern car manufacturing. Cars are highly complex products produced by highly structured processes. In most instances products of high quality result. When something does go wrong, however, it is not unusual for a company to recall 100,000 or 200,000 vehicles to correct the problem. There are no 'little mistakes'.

The second concern is that within a short period of time, organizationally, the process becomes the purpose. Standardized processes are developed to achieve a consistent result efficiently, whether it is the production of a good or the provison of a service. The welfare of those individuals within the process is directly tied to that process. Vary from the process and suffer negative economic consequences, i.e. lose your job. Compliance with the standardized process represents security, i.e. do what you are told and they will not fire you. Attempting to alter the process represents personal risk.

Compliance with the process represents not only personal security, but organizational and financial success. Individuals learn the 'Organizational Way' and by following that process, they move up within the organization. Over time, organizational leaders build their careers on the process. They enforce the organizational process to the exclusion of alternatives. The product or service is ultimately subordinated to compliance with the process. **The process becomes the purpose of the organization.**

Let me provide an example; a private sector company is founded with the development of a new process to cut costs provide additional services in a new and more efficient manner. If the process is successful, over a period of time, it becomes just as institutionalized. Books are written about the secrets of their success in the market place: 'The GE Way', 'The Ford Way'. Each book praising the process which brought success to the organization it describes. The process becomes the purpose.

In the 1950s many companies used direct mail solicitation

to sell their products. Mail was the standard way of communicating across long distances; telephone was much too expensive; radio and TV were still seen as methodologies for advertizing consumables. The opening rate of unsolicited mail ran approximately 10%.

As the 21st century dawned some delivery channels declined in cost and new ones appeared. The opening rate of unsolicited mail declined to less than 1%, and the cost per item increased. Various steps were taken to improve delivery, including new strategies in targeting and design but the truth was clear; alternative means of message delivery were much more cost effective.

Still, for many organizations, direct mail was part of their success in the 1950s and that process was institutionalized. They still send direct mail because they had always gotten their customers that way. It does not need to make economic sense: the process had become the purpose. Academics refer to this as organizational atrophy.

A similar organizational development pattern occurs in public sector organizations, an example of atrophy is the lessons of Napoleon Bonaparte. Napoleon successfully introduced new processes into the art of war. Quickly making strategic moves, dividing his enemies, he introduced the massed bayonet charge where thousands of Frenchmen would simply carry the day by quickly closing the distance with their enemies and driving them from the field by the weight of sheer numbers. Over years of fighting Napoleon taught Europe and the world a new process of war.

From 1814 to 1914, armies across the world, studied and applied the lessons Napoleon taught. Military cadets were commissioned and promoted based upon their understanding and application of Napoleonic tactics. Individuals who questioned the process, were passed over for promotion or simply removed from service. The process had become the purpose and was not to be questioned - organizational atrophy.

As time passed Napoleonic tactics became increasingly less effective, but still the organizations (armies) held fast to the basic process. If the lessons of Napoleon did not work, some other factor must be at fault. The carnage of the American Civil War, with mass bayonet charges against rifles and breach loading cannon, was not seen by European analysts as a failure of Napoleonic tactics but rather a failure of the American warrior.

In 1917, after a million men had died, the soldiers of the French Army grew tired of charging German machine guns with their bayonets and mutinied. Almost 40% of the French army refused to follow orders to attack. The French High Command believing the failure could not be the fault of the 100-year-old Napoleonic tactics but rather concluded the failure was the fault of 'cowardice' in the ranks and considered having every tenth man shot. It was a classic example of organizational atrophy.

There is a major difference of organizational atrophy between the private sector and the public sector. In the private sector, when an organization atrophies, it isn't long before it ceases to exist. Organizations which once had been thriving American businesses such as the Barnum & Bailey, Sears, and Blockbuster, all failed and passed out of existence. The key to their success, their processes, had become their purpose, and they were unable to recognize and adapt to the changing environment.

In the public sector, the result of process stagnation is much different. The public sector utilizes the power of coercion (taxes) to gain revenue. A decline in the efficiency of the process results in an increasing demand for resources (taxes) to accomplish the same purpose. (I am convinced that half the conversations in government start with the sentence 'If we only had a few more assets.')

The private company which sees the efficiency of its

marketing program decline by 50% can end up with the same result simply by doubling the marketing budget. Of course, at some point, the marketing becomes so expensive the company can no longer survive.

But the public sector does not have that problem. The public sector is not constrained by the free exchange of goods and services by which the private sector is constrained. The less efficient governmental programs are, the more people they employ. If the efficiency of agovernmental program declines by 50%, the public sector simply doubles the money spent and often doubles the number of employees; there are no economic constraints.

The private sector is a constantly bubbling cauldron of creative destruction. Organizations are created, grow, atrophy, and die. The constant search for new products, services, and efficiencies makes new fortunes and destroys old ones. The public sector is the inverse; using its monopoly of power, it locks out change, ensuring atrophy and inefficiencies. Process became purpose and Blockbuster Inc. went bankrupt. Process became purpose in 19th century French Army and millions of French soldiers died in the 20th century.

In the private economic sector, the process is subordinate to the purpose, or the organization dies. In the public sector, the process becomes the purpose and the bureaucracy grows.

The Process Improvement Handbook: A Blueprint for Managing Change and Increasing Organizational Performance
Publisher: McGraw-Hill Education; 1 edition (October 15, 2013)
ISBN-10: 0071817662, ISBN-13: 978-0071817660

Chapter 11

Atrophy & Collapse

'It would be a bitter cosmic joke if we destroy ourselves due to atrophy of the imagination.' - Martha Gellhorn

Politicians keep finding new 'goods' to promote. Each new good requires an extension of the bureaucracy. The bureaucracy independently expands its original mission in scope, requiring additional assets to accomplish those self-assigned goals. Through Civil Service and public unions members of the bureaucracy are almost impervious to improvement.

The effects of Parkinson's Law, The Peter Principle, Process Attrophy, and the lack of creators within a normal Pareto Distribution compound one another and ensure an increasingly inefficient bureaucracy. They require additional assets to accomplish explicitly and implicitly assigned tasks.

'One of the greatest threats to mankind today is that the world may be choked by an explosively pervading but well camouflaged bureaucracy.' - Norman Borlaug

Bureaucracies do not create wealth. They are expensive, parasitic, and at very best they reallocate the wealth others create while deducting a significant percentage of that wealth for itself. As the bureaucracy expands, the expense of a bureaucracy increases, while the number of actual creators within the society declines. Some individuals give up on the private sector and join the public sector. Others, Pareto's creators, simply flee the country compounding the problem by taking productivity with them. Ultimately the monster, which is the bureaucracy, grows in size and inefficiency to the point at which it provides only highly limited services to the country it is supposed to be serving. Inflated government extracts high taxes and provides little benefit.

The Laffer Curve is a theory developed by Dr. Arthur Laffer showing the relationship between tax rates and the amount of tax revenue collected by governments; i.e. there is an optimum tax rate, beyond which actual government revenue declines.

If the government imposes no taxes, then the government receives no tax revenue. If the government imposes a

100% tax rate, the government again receives no tax revenue because no one will work for free. As the government bureaucracy grows, the tax rate goes up to support that bureaucracy.

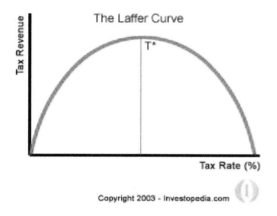

The flip side to this coin is that, as the tax rate goes up and it becomes more difficult to make a living, the number of people desiring to join the bureaucracy goes up! Financial security is very attractive when compared to the risks of a highly taxed private sector.

'Getting things done in this country, if you want to build something, if you want to start a company, it's getting to be virtually impossible with all of the bureaucracy and all of the approvals.' - Donald Trump

One particularly ugly aspect of the approaching failure is

George E. Anderson, III, PhD

the bureaucracies' behavior during its final days. Typically, the economy has collapsed for lack of creators and wild expenses for an unproductive government. To protect the system they are a part of members of the bureaucracy will resort to violence, and ultimately murder against those they are supposed to be serving. This has been repeated in the last days of almost every socialist government and is currently going on in Venezuela.

The Decline and Fall of the Roman Empire, Edward Gibbon ISBN-13: 978-0307700766, ISBN-10: 0307700763

Chapter 12

Hope

'My dream is of a place and a time where America will once again be seen as the last best hope of earth.' - Abraham Lincoln

In his seminal work, *The Structure of Scientific Revolutions*, Thomas S. Kuhn described the steps the academic community goes through prior to any major change in scientific thought. That same pattern occurs in changing any organizational process. The concept (and the resulting actions) are institutionalized, lessons are taught, and careers are made on the basis of embracing the accepted belief. As the concepts (and resulting actions) begin to decline in efficacy, the theory is 'tweaked' to fit the new reality. It is only after complete failure that a search for an alternative concept is begun. That process of change holds true in the scientific community as well as the business community and the public arena.

America has not been exempted from the phenomenon of

an ever growing, ever more inefficient bureaucracy. The politician's siren call to make things ever better and the resluting ever-growing bureaucracy can challenge even an extraordinarily wealthy country such as the United States.

'We have met the enemy and he is us.' — Walt Kelly (Pogo)

Turning away in the most recent election from hollow promises of a benevolent state selflessly caring for the population, should give all Americans hope. America was born on the concept of individual liberty, not government security. Americans have sacrificed and died since our founding to ensure liberty for themselves and their posterity. Liberty, not security, made the United States the richest country in the history of humankind. Liberty, with all its variances, successes, and failures, is what makes the United States the shining beacon on the hill.

We do not have to face the fate of socialist countries. It is not too late. Remember. Americans are citizens not subjects. The government is there to protect our liberty, not to provide us cell phones.

'The greatness of America lies not in being more enlightened than any other nation, but rather in her ability to repair her faults.' - Alexis de Tocqueville

Addendum

I lied. There is actually a scenario in which socialism has proven it can work for an extended period of time. For such a system to 'work' two factors must be in place. First, the population needs to be small and homogeneous. This lack of size and social complexity allows the country to answer the question 'What is good?' The second criterion is that the country must have significant, perhaps even vast national (sovereign) assets with which to fund the created programs without impoverishing some individuals for the benefit of other individuals. Thus, a country like Norway can agree on what is good and because of the revenue from North Sea oil, can afford it.

For the rest of the world, where those two criteria are not present, Socialism does not work because socialism cannot work.

George E. Anderson, III, PhD

ABOUT THE AUTHOR

George E Anderson holds a BA in History from The Citadel, The Military College of South Carolina, a MS in Management from the University of Southern California and a PhD in Organization and Management from Capella University. He has taught business at both the undergraduate and the graduate levels. A decorated retired veteran, his award winning academic articles have been published in 42 languages across the globe. Dr. Anderson examines the structural factors which have brought failure to every attempt at a government-controlled economy. **Socialism does not work because socialism cannot work.**

George E. Anderson, III, PhD

Printed in Great Britain
by Amazon

82289620R00048